The Squatters' Gift

Robert Rybicki

THE SQUATTERS' GIFT

Translated from the Polish by Mark Tardi

DALKEY ARCHIVE PRESS
Dallas / Dublin

Originally published in Polish as *Dar Meneli*, 2017
Copyright © 2018 by Robert Rybicki and Biuro Literackie
Translation copyright © 2021 by Mark Tardi
Cover art copyright © by Lula Bajek

First Dalkey Archive edition, 2021

ISBN: 9781628973730
CIP Data available upon request.

www.dalkeyarchive.com
Dallas / Dublin

Printed on permanent/durable acid-free paper.

Translator's Note

Born in Rybnik, Poland in 1976, Robert "Ryba" Rybicki is a one-person cosmopolis and, over the past two decades, his status within his native Poland has grown to near-mythic proportions. A self-described "happener," Rybicki creates poetic events as he works at the intersection of performance and disruption, theatricality and confrontation, going back to figures such as Rolf Brinkmann, Tadeusz Kantor, and Stanisław ("Witkacy") Witkiewicz. He is the author of nine books, including *Epifanie i katatonie* [Epiphanies & Catatonics], *Masakra kalaczakra* [Kalachakra massacre], and *Podręcznik naukowy dla onironautów* [A Scientific Handbook for Oneironauts].

His award-winning book *The Squatters' Gift* is a poetic travelogue through numerous languages and locales, both real and imaginary. Like Miron Białoszewski, Paul Celan, and Tristan Tzara before him, Rybicki excavates syllable and song, mind and muck, to invent a transnational poetry pointedly unapologetic and utterly unique. Karol Maliszewski observes that Rybicki has taken over from the Surrealists and the Dadaists: "the hero of these poems is language — escaping from a man and suddenly returning in flashes and dazzles. Some of these dazzles are of the highest quality, withstanding comparisons to the dazzles of Max Jacob or Rene Char."

When I first read the opening lines of the poem "The shots will disappear," which begins *The Squatters' Gift*, I was struck with the impression that I was encountering a sort of vagabond Jack Gladney from Don DeLillo's acclaimed *White Noise*, wandering the supermarket aisles in a consumerist haze: "The supermarket / melts / like a chocolate bar: / a dendrite stack." But the comparison was short-lived, an illusionary foothold that proved far too simplistic. The Gladney connection is only tenable if the comforts of ritualized shopping are multilingual and multidimensional, Greek mythology intersecting with 1980s Polish punk music, poetic string theory, time travel, and psychedelic dumpster diving all rolled into one. Amidst the current global pandemic where so many of us are largely sheltering-in-place, the wanderlust and imaginative leaps that animate much of *The Squatters' Gift* seem all the more incredible.

Rybicki navigates radical and acrobatic shifts in style and register, macro- and micro-scale. Although they work in different media, the visual artist Gerhard Richter is a reasonable comparison: both figures can effortlessly slide between vocabularies and formal gestures that are neoclassical, romantic, realist, or more avant-garde works that are highly conceptualized and abstract. While Richter does so pictorially, Rybicki's medium is language—longitudinally and latitudinally. In *The Squatters' Gift*, Rybicki's poetic speakers direct and misdirect the reader through the frictions of multiple languages convening and conversing, sometimes imploding from profound deformations of syntax or sense. For Rybicki, "Poetry's / the mathematics of / an inaccessible / dimension."

Like Rybicki himself, the poems in *The Squatters' Gift* are peripatetic, passing through—and sometimes squatting in—Gliwice, Wrocław, Poznań, Prague, Vienna, Bratislava, Rybnik, Kraków, Warsaw, Toruń, Gdańsk, Świnoujście, and Lublin. Just as the speakers shift locales, so do the poems' subjects and forms. And while Rybicki writes primarily in Polish, he freely uses Czech, English, French, German, Spanish, Slovak, and Silesian dialect throughout his work. To impose consistency on a poetry so far-reaching is a fool's errand. Maciek Woźniak sees Rybicki's poems as reflective "not of crystallized views or fortified as religious dogmas [. . .] but a free-thinking spirit, usually condemned to (and for) vagrancy." The linguistic grabs and volleys in Rybicki's work is challenging to the extreme: some aspects of the Silesian dialect, for example, were all but impossible to render into English, since I did not wish anybody to confuse Rybicki for Jar Jar Binks. The German and Spanish in his poems, however, have largely been untouched.

Poet and critic Adam Wiedemann suggests that it's as if Rybicki begins each poem "at the zero point of poetry" and continues "without respecting sacred literary rules and especially 'culture.'" Not unlike American poet Michael Palmer, contradictory impulses animate Rybicki's poetics, as he continuously toggles between the epistemic and the somatic. As he writes in *The Squatters' Gift*, "Thought clamps the body / like a barrel rim." These competing modes allow Rybicki at one moment to offer poems that recall Adam Mickiewicz's *Crimean Sonnets* or Czesław Miłosz while at another embodying the wide-reaching iconoclasm of Peter Handke's *Offending the Audience on Purpose*. Antoni Zając suggests that being uncompromisingly anti-dogmatic "is perhaps the essence of Robert Rybicki's poetry." Or as Maciej Woźniak aptly explains:

> The Squatters' Gift allows you to look at the fundamental contradiction driving Rybicki's work: extreme individualism collides with social empathy, radical skepticism and situational ethics with the community spirit and leftist sensitivity. Gorgias meets Christ, Socrates — Jacek Kuroń. Poems, whose arena is the poetic 'I' . . . also become attempts to elevate linguistic foundations for a new interpersonal reality. Sophisticated poetic paradoxes are not stairs up to a literary Olympus, but in the opposite direction — because the direction towards clarity and purity turns out to be down.

Rybicki's poems actively resist stasis and are buttressed by myriad neologisms and elisions, which can make getting a stable *feel* for the writing both disorienting and liberating. Whether in an abandoned, overgrown stadium or a cobblestoned alleyway, swimming over a coral reef or imagining the geometry of the Big Bang, Rybicki's lines move. These poems can change locations, languages and layouts at breakneck speed or the speaker can slow down to marvel at polygons or puke. Buckminster Fuller once wrote, "We're all astronauts on a little spaceship called Earth," to which Rybicki could retort "the heavens aren't silent / if you have them in you."

Mark Tardi
June 2020, Poland

Contents

I.

II. A New Tristan Tzara Urgently Needed

III. ROTOROBERTEIL*

* Titles marked with an asterisk have been unchanged from the original Polish edition.

The Squatters' Gift

The shots will disappear

The supermarket
melts   like a chocolate bar:
            a dendrite stack. *Somebody*, with a chic scarf
      around her neck, rearranges   tissues, sighs.
Don't   I have anything?
                        dialectic tendons. Drugs.
      Whale brains on the conveyor belt.   (un marinero)
Satyrs passed the dialogue   a volleyball.
                  Dreams circled like hawks.
Down the vines   of verses the vervets
of words   disappear in a jungle of meanings, *their*
howls bounce off   the foliage.   a diagram.
                  veiled horse-frogs. Microfrankenstein.
            scrutiny   & *vice versa*.
                  I was 16 years old once.   (historial médico)
                              High quality
visibility,

                  bioethics,   computer.
            awareness enabled
like night vision,

                                          (el dirigible)
      a waterfall plunges from the roof of Mrówkowiec[1],
                        leftovers of **yellow** paint
the man wasn't arranged
in parallel,   a surplus of impressions after a lavish day.
      he swam over a coral reef,
      glowing viscera   translucent ribs
            the fossil of olympic nectar.

---

[1] Mrówkowiec (Ant Farm Estates) is an enormous eleven-story building erected in Wrocław in the mid-1960s which houses some two-thousand residents in nearly six-hundred apartments.

A hesitation after passing the Pillars
of Hercules,
                                        a sheaf
              of electric sparks in the abysses of the brain:
        lightning between the synapses
                                                      fruit

     of a funny misunderstanding
                    faith in a deeper failure.
          inside the brain,
                    wind into the nervous system.
             over the span of the bridge from Bristol
to Newport,
        a hydroelectric plant,
                                        yourself unreflected
in the water
              the thumb   after vanishing.

        a stained-glass brain in the rosette of the skull.
                                                      the
more embarrassed that I'm still talking.
                              Scanner,
                                        now you're a diode.

        infinity swells like
a balloon.   blossoms,   swells,

              a semi-breathing form of life,
        beam of dimensions

from its own impassable center,
          like some medieval work,
                    lemme have a drink
of anchors' brew,
                    tassels of hair were flowing down the window

4

     the porter dragged a tired donkey
in the soul of the Trabant
                the chip fell, the monk
scuffled among the yataghans
                   The Automat's Brother.
          slithered into the dark den,
                      with faded sequins.
My crosshairs broke,   frozen tortes

          the Terminator with a bunch of keys to
crack the cryptogram.
I knelt to tie a shoelace,
                 like a sick apple leaf. Tubers
of Words.
a bunch of stratified vegetables. I picked up
          a cracked clam shell,
the runway for a sluggish fly.
In a glass   a tea stone from a thousand years ago.
I saw Genghis Khan's army   on motorcycles.
          an old sprocket.
              over the grass of proverbs.
              the majorette, twirling
a baton,   the moon is shining.
I can only divine   the half silence

          I saw the tombstones of medieval bishops.
faces flat like plates,
          a canopy of cross-ribbed
vaults

          we'll pass   under the sky-high portal,
       a sculpted history   of dreams strung together.
       after connecting   to the integrated circuit, which
          mindless coagulation

the cybernetic ecstasy
with heart
rate   of the paradox of existence.
         a generator powered by the gyrations of the solar system.

the smell of burnt flesh from the chest.
         by the blast furnaces,
                  it's good that they weren't human bones.

I'm coming to you, my missed opportunities,
                  via particles of humid
air during a storm, an anchor made of fragile
palm
glass,   the frosty
herald of a chimerical autumn,

         burn, experiences,   in the heap of Words.

Dunk sans bunk

the violet Volkswagen   the vitality of Ricky.
    Oh, marsh mermaid,   poviat weekends.
     at a stall with souvenirs & white arms,
      near the tram terminus,

     she sends a rocket full of tears,
impersonal tears,   tears that don't need tariffs
           dead sparrow.
the concert crowd
Harps of ribs.

           in the landfill of traumas
     mycobacteria mold.
the bunk of fulfillment

in the middle of nowhere by a stream—CCTV.
Reading is a way to cover your face.
        Brass flemingos.

Crab claws in the air! Anarchy in the forest! Electro-ego!

'Tis the season — the smell of shit & earth. The whoosh of mast lines with flags.
In such cases, you need a plan that'll throw
rhetoric off-balance;
       rhetoric like a fog in a landfill of Myth.
It was supposed to be natural speech but we ended up with liminal speech.
When I warm up to a girl, she goes home.

Here's a phrase at midnight: the vines wrap around the terrace and, it seems,

start to replace the suspenders, the fog once more, of diluted
thoughts, dandelions in the stomach.

A comma between *beginning* and *end*.

I think only singing unites word with body
when you return home thru the dogma,
the jungle.

Fan of embers

Saliva shines on the sidewalk.

a uni urinal.

She hasn't finished her cigarette yet,
but she's already finished talking.

the rippling receipt
the patches of sweat

Thought clamps the body
like a barrel rim.

A bum's crisp, clear voice
emerges from the rumble,

Only the knocking of heads
against the tables reached my blunt ears
when I tried to
concentrate on a single word,
which came as if from afar, from
across the sea, crystalline,
strained
from obligations,
unconditional

& the whole courtyard's paved
with judges' skulls, whose
logic has failed.

the ruts will lead you to the conclusion

Myth has been roaming since its journey began.

                                                           life

rests, breathing
at a tidal rate

The starting point for
thoughts,
thought Myth.

the cornea dampens

underwater, self-conscious,
on the seabed, when
we were rolled toward each other
by the restless
sea of language into
the mouth of the bay, the jagged-
tongued cape, when the bodies were
reducing their volume, keeping proportions
in balance

of water to the body weight
of speech, when we exhaled
more than we inhaled,
turning into jellyfish,
our stingers deep in the water,
water speech,

and your every word
was like a rising tide.

Then I shyly
crawled ashore.

It's impossible to stop doubting
people when you exist.

　　　　(THEY'RE AFRAID
　　　　of everything, losing
　　　　control, you must have
　　　　control over
　　　　something, no
　　　　thing.
　　　　　　　　Poetry's
　　　　the mathematics of
　　　　an inaccessible
　　　　dimension ((. . .)

is contained
in the cosmos —
& before that
the pulsating heart
of the sun, which pumps
the blood of the new week,
nourished & shiny.

　　　　And
before that,
you.)

A logorithm

where the filming of ego
takes real form &
he becomes but an accessory
to his facial expressions

as if he wanted to scour the grain
on the paneling of a gazdówka[2]

instead of a montage
a storm trailer screened across the sky,
a photo session with the clouds
the experimental rustling of the rain

IN THE LIGHTNING
THEATRE

elemental mathematics

to summon people with your eyes

A word that can hurl against the walls,
against the walls!

We experience the joy of existence,
saying goodbye to the fact
that we're already long gone.

---

[2] Gazdówka: wooden houses in the Polish Zakopane style popularized by Stanisław "Witkacy" Witkiewicz.

We've come
to the first spark of existence
& feel the joy
that a new being has emerged aflame.

When reason is crazy,
focus is incalculable
in the face of facts.

The horizon is our common idea.
Universe, there is no horizon.

Will there be enough fear for words
which — exhausted — are returning from the dark?
Who called them with a cry from sleep?

Nobody, the shadow of an amorphous
dusts memories over a song sung by a dirty voice,
the wind howls right through him!

Who — sucked in the turbine
of a space propeller —
will be a boundless flame?

Oh, tired words,
steel gray flame!

—the splattered spruce   gray leaf claws
on the metal dial   the giggle of bones
beyond the timeline —   at the pink hour

                                              at dawn, at dawn
                                              the force at dawn

MAN, SPEECH & IMPOTENCE

Preason. Swamingo.
Wristulla between pincers, in the chackles.
out of nowswhere, down with it.
With the human rea
soning.

A knownot, fraction. Tuny.

　　　Gim your hand. Bow brow
　　　to another, the other —

　　　"respect"
　　　"modern."

The inverted songpits
Agh awashed with mo. Of lamps.

Mothness. Unspokement. A block.
It's an unbreakon lan. Break

yoursell. Yell. Where's he
fromm. An unvile

tongue unobtained from the viscera,
ununfound, flashy, fleshy,
reckless in the extracts from its nature,
feckless in the descriptions of the blind,
though kind, inclined and refined;

in the prosody of perdition
in the music of martyrdom,

secretly give yourself
an answer. Without experti.

2.

Towers,
spires,
chimneys,
sky
scrapers.

Concrete,
brick,
walls
of glass.

Ten-story
apartment buildings.

At the feet
& from up high.

On the side of the road,
in the woods,

all the same.

3.

A blue
signpost in sleepy ivy,
when twilight lays a shadow
on an orange
display,
        & the month
was violent, like an avalanche,
while it could have been like a waterfall,
steady. The journey became a mound
& in its inertia:
             Spoken
in a prison of sentences; at the same time
I found a muzzle in the gazebo,

when a pigeon pressed into the asphalt
                      took off
into asphodels.

4.

Behold the man who wiped out on a balloon.
When he was hungry, his thoughts were clear.
He remembers others, but not himself.
He doesn't talk about all that, only exists.
In the morning, a shadow of

memory throws him a wink—or so he thinks;
but he always knows what the day will hold
when at dawn, he stifles a yawn &
then hoists himself up like a pawn:

piss off!

GREAT WIRES

quagmires
& shaking
landslides,

see you in 30 seconds
or 7,000 years.

The electric pigeon
smelled the stink of the burning potato rootstock.

In the middle of nowhere, a trailer full of taters.

The ur-stink.

2.

I'm a puppetto under the plane of fate
Ramses is from Rydułtowy,

he's in for a bow-tied talking-to
in the stink of burning taters.
The poviat oligarchy resembles a square
of corn in the middle of nowhere,
at night, suddenly

on a walking trip from Rybnik to Gliwice
at night, suddenly
these 25 km become a godsend
in the blinding glow of halogens in the fog,

the darkness of
darknesses.

The ground underfoot is all.
A backpack framed by the car lights' shimmer,
& in the memory a square full of offices,
whose names appearing in the phrase
would be unpleasant to the ear,

while existential weightlessness
fills every cell of the body —
or wood, to be precise. They said:

> *"Look, this guy was about to jump off*
> *the stratosphere, and since yesterday*
> *it's been on Wikipedia!"*

3.

I heard the vocal
from *Nowa Aleksandria*[3],
it sucked. Corn,
thirteen cobs,
occupy the eyes at the entrance
to the tiny kitchen.

In a glass, LUBUSKI
((GIN) NEVEЯ?), which,
going up from the "square"
bottom, is rounded
at the mouth (for the leftovers
of ginger & cinnamon tea)

---

[3] *Nowa Alexandria* was a 1986 album from the Polish post-punk band Siekiera ("Axe" in English) released on the Tonpress record label.

the teaspoon dances
with intricate, fine
decorations, from the base
to the handle, à la acanthus,
the inscription, blurred, be it Latin or

Русский, but the tapping of
this teaspoon was neither horse
hooves nor an element
of percussion, it wasn't
a hand, it did it by itself —

    — & on vocals,
    Siwy and Adala? —

4. peacock among people

T
shirt, *shit, fuck*, donde está
la heladería, the world
having fallen out of the revolution of the self,
woke up, the first phrase

was supposed to be like a spliff's tip,
& what's below should sprawl,

lay low until the d-d-difficult days come,
& the wasps fly lower & lower, the doggy
ran & yanked his fang on the jeans to

be with people & have doubts.

When will I stop dreaming
about the fucks from Greek mythology?

And when will I remember the words
that ran off into oblivion?
        (It's cool, clever, intense
        like a glass of ginger water
        or a volume with a B&W cover)
This washing machine has lost its fucking mind
        while he ran across the city
        & portals to other worlds opened up.

Why did I dream of a villa   And on the other side, another villa
full of American poets?   full of British poets?

A yawning face in a sharp chiaroscuro is a reflected glass pane.
Who gave you a designate?
Do you assume anything?

The sea glued to bread.

A plain of stupidity.

Insert and eject verses like drawers
full of flies or twist ties—

                                        with a thunderbolt inside.

Here's an estate of vacant wall-less prefabs.
Smile to a flower, get your lollypop & go there.

A Nobody waits there. Next to him, a red diode
        splattered across the shiny crossroads

                                of metal structures,

that float like balloons—

                          your eyes like blimps
                                on towers' spires.

The highway covered with blackened sunflowers.

A man with a beard like thistle. Buddy-buds.

Lanucy. Nocho. A Gummi bear bites at the camra.
Faith makes the deuterium. Sodium lamps
of consciousness. What the fuck are you talking about,
sheepman, an avalanche of sound. Feces
worth its weight in gold & truth.
Rattle me up, swing my bits.
Click me in the ground, bone against
the stone, a pigeon falls down, speechless.
The coughing date keeps unclipping like a skyscraper
keyring of a kid's bawl. Crying
has a talent. Blood rumbles & shines,
gets reflected on the beat-up
film of memory, scratched-up photographic
membrane, the mucosa of horror,
numbered telephones linger, three
hours a day, eight hours
a day, the week is burning, give it
magnesium, give it light, not
the nightlight, not the sun or the moon,
though it's in full, not the eye, has
anyone seen an invisible light,
concealed by knowing, a light
from a different dimension, has
anyone seen it, it pours inside the self,
Nobody sees, the name disappears, the word
recedes, the rhythm is suspended,

the dreams about nows, the idea in
the light, the end, purity, unity,
flight is no longer needed,
plight is no longer needed,
there's no shape,
no contour,
permeated,
pervaded,
no matter,
no text.

Like a hand without a signature,
the Mannequin of Gravitas
opens its mouth to you.

JOURNEY AROUND THE STATION

A drop on the needle, but
something like the crack of a board against the cobbles &
the laughter of three girls
on a soundless walk as

vitrified snow &
lumpenbroletariat

among the polystyrene butterflies
& files of memory dumps system errors
& dream like dawn:

not only the stomach & liver
are hungry. The arms are hungry.
And every beginning's bracketed by banality,
like, for example, communist absolutism,
& this *And* at the beginning of the sentence, hard
to swallow. Is this —
a cheatsheet with burns? Burn yourself.

He sits as if he wasn't there
but is in the game. Follows
the blast of events,
got blown off the event to somewhere.
Soon, after a while, he will stretch indefinitely.

A drop on the needle
became a blaze
shredding the eyes;
the projector streak directly

thru the pupil, into the eyeball,
what film's being played
in the brain? What was cut off?

Wind board? Whooping
laughter? Rumpled?
Yo, light! Come be!

Some,

what. Somewhat
& nowise. Smothering.

Geometry be a thing of the past
with an explosion of nothingness
that unfolds,

cleaves,

deprivation. A flash
of stupidity, unrequested, &
this maybe be a construct. Nothing
being. Nothing's
off the leash.

Visits of emptiness.
Emptiness visits the night.
Detours from sleep, toward
            clear
            vision

what appears
beyond the senses
as natural,
consorting
soundless,
necessary,

unlimited

(type "so"
& the program suggests:

"soaring")

Hum,

hum, buzz,
buzz.
X-ray of a word,
x-ray of a word,
persistently
not repeat
& reproduce,
move away
& return again.
Near,
far:
round forms.
I'll conform
to the word,
which itself
has been implanted,

as if searching
to find the
scope of
this thing.

Somethink.

To the edge of knowledge!

"knowing."

The. Word. Rotates. Like. A. Tornado.

All. Constructions. Thoughts.
Like. Exhibits. In. A. Museum.

In one moment

two thoughts flew thru the brain
& left streaks
like jets. In
the narrowness of an answer,
in the constraint of an answer
to all ills, to
this one question, which
is always one question
regardless of circumstances, when
the letter "c" doesn't pop up when
pressed, any
pressing as an atavistic form of vitality (au revoir,
academic jargon!)

none of you, university schmunts,
can mess with my poem.

I saw an echo of thoughts.
Thought sent a wave that
bounced off something
certainly not off the skull,
certainly not off the rock wall,
certainly not from a you reading
critically, which is also a figure
in this
line. Maybe
it's a Hungarian, hung

in the chute, in shambles
I, which envelops in you,
beyond the romantic

conditions of love,
beyond all conventions,
beyond the hope for change,
beyond change.

Recently, I read lectures by Michel Foucault & there it was
plain as day:

get to know yourself,
take care of yourself.

To Swallow a Shadow—

these words are
nothing more than
tobacco specks
on a sheet of paper
(a mouth full of skeletons);
me, out of my head,
like a ball rolling towards the pocket.

A dog's tongue,
saliva; the trace
of existence.

So many thoughts,
over & over,
until he holes up in his head,
as if he were dreamed up by his tongue.

From reproduction to contemplation:
steppes & mountain ranges.

Words, devoured
by intention
lose their dignity;

a thought
chewed over
till you're chucking, tho still steady
in intersecting
gales of snow   snów
slow   słów

& this poor I,
excluded from its power,

standing at the gate
                OF THE GREAT CONTAINERYARD
forgotten,
which used to have a name & form

HUNTING FOR OSWALD EGGER[4]

I got double-fucking-dragoned
                    in Bratislava
& was going to Vienna with a black eye,
with an idea on how to spell Lviv's ł
(łł) & I thought:
                    fuck these shitbirds

when *theirs* was everything I owned
except my backpack,

& since I was drunk,
I didn't think:
                    how the fuck will I look with this bitch under my eye
in a turquoise-lemon sweatshirt
from the duty-free shop in Praha?

                    Honza
is surely getting off now

Didi & Vašo no different

Oswald Egger & Rolf Dieter Brinkmann[5]
collided in one head
                    ELEKTRISCHE ZÄUNE
after all, I've been to Auschwitz three times
                    & how are you supposed to write poetry after Oświęcim,

---

[4] Oswald Egger — Italian-born writer who lived much of his life in Vienna, Austria and is currently professor of Language and Form at Muthesius University of Art and Design, Kiel.

[5] Rolf Dieter Brinkmann (1940–1975) was an anti-establishment German writer of poems, short stories, a novel, essays, letters, and diaries who died in London.

sitting at the Bibliothek Von Unten,[6]
& in Praha, (A) VOID GALLERIE[7]
      & Petr Motýl[8] complaining about the situation
      in the Czech book market;
      & rightly so, similar to Polish publishers.

At EKH[9]
a festival of Czech bands from punk to hard core,

a odkud jste, I've won 90%

of the foosball matches &
after a good bit of chalk,
      I discovered a talent for billiards . . .

they look at me here like I'm an alien
but can you blame them
a looney from Poland
with a black eye
in search of Oswald Egger,
& he,
      as claimed by Hans & Gerhard
while I hit my stride drinking
RED WINE,
      lives
      in Deutschland, am Nord,
What the fucking what? — I screamed — *Was? nicht in Wien?*
until Silvia[10] came
& I went with her.

---

[6] Anarchist's library in Vienna.

[7] A gallery on a boat on the River Vltava in Prague

[8] Petr Motýl (b. 1964), Czech poet born in the Czech part of Silesia who lives in Prague.

[9] Ernst-Kirchweger-Haus is a building in Vienna near the Wien Hauptbahnhof railway station that had been squatted for two decades.

[10] Silvia Ruppeldtová, a respected Slovak translator who translates from six languages.

EXCERPTS FROM BRINKMANN

—to be alien-like
        to yourself;
actually: you can
        (*kann man*)
        meet someone
in poetry.   Thoughts met in spite
        of the languages!

In the hall
of   the   new ly   built
                    sta tion (Ö
BB[11]) I reckoned: a fist
            can't beat love.

Those who have a gun
            only use it for one purpose: TO KILL

(every man who has a gun
is a terrorist to *me*)

Ah, these Austrian woemens,

                none
                will read me
                four poems
                in the morning
                for breakfast.

---

[11] Austrian railway

Stress, the cemented square,
sagte Brinkmann. The city,
centered to gray,
is like a filthy asshole.

With travels ahead,
having crossed, when

ktereho jazyka použivat?:
how do people
who spend time
in one place feel,
                    in one city,
                        one town?

How does Waldemar Jocher[12] feel?

A PRISON OF PLACE
                    OF LANGUAGE
                        OF IDENTITY

---

[12] Waldemar Jocher (b. 1970), a Polish poet from Prudnik.

How

to translate yourself
into language, flip
inside out
with it, where
those who feel cramped
in this world, can make it

                                             &

how will the language flip us
once we're indifferent?

WHEN

power
be ininternalized,
"as" something that comes from the outside, cast
like a net
     over "I"; &
               when
"the said"
                   net from the outside
be inside &
"what" wants to be free
but is parceled out
     by the "structure" —
     of what's "cast"
          "pushed"
     inside,
             allows
to be expressed, "pressed"; shred.

               "This"
"normativized"
"normalized"
               "I"

be horseshit,

     that be not power,
     even a dumpster
          is laughing its ass off

f yuck , the word
                              pulls
for the hole after
                              the bullet wound,
the head no longer holds anything,
            the head is a hotbed,

a landfill of unnecessary memories,
            a cluttered room.

only in a "foreign" language
the "native" tongue is a sling

& this "I" "gives"
let it stay

outside "necessity"
                     "obligation"

as a law
      for unrestrict
      ed handouts,

when a pen
      does
      a fucking salto mortale
      und pirouette

& "this" b-boying
                     of thoughts
run over
by a transgalactic roller,
                              a rolling pin

& fiery lips
with frozen speech,

& a begging attitude
against the certainty
of ownership, & the one

"I"
be a memory of power.

HAPPY DADA:

gada dorada, jsem
viděla hada, nie lada
zwada zwała się estrada
    i była psem,
    a do rana Praga
    o rany, krk, reggae
trh a krb! Skrada się Saddam
do Muhammada po grass
            i bada
       czy pada
deszcz
als happy dada als sound'da,
    to nie wada Pounda,
a woda doda nam sił,
ku temu pogoda,
        gdy dodo gnił,
gdy anoda i katoda nic nam nie doda,
gdy nada się na nic nie nada
und null mit nuddeln in moon,
      pagoda i dynamiczny skun,
skok in school, skeptic kung-fu in typhoon,
           und simpsons on screen
               w doktryn

      dodawaniu dna do dalszych den
i godo: mur nur fur kur
         ciul-dup.
No-one knows how it grows,
frazofrenik z fraktalem frędzla fryzury Freuda,
ale fala z woala à la Aal im Allee,

sallam fallus
als minulost,

co ona gada w tym anglodada,
czarna čočka w ciemnościach ćmi

ako die

i Didi i MIDI LIDI
und da:
nomada gada dada
als Versager

la palabra el
elefante
telefantom
Cimo ni mo
synonimo
telebimo
bunco beardo
maybe baby can-
do nicely
dolphin doobie
en paradiso
& a face
so sprightly
in solidarity
let him come
to the N1 &
she said lesen
& electro
einbaumöbel
warm wine
all the time
sha-sha-shaman
& Socrates
Schwamm und Sprache

poetry must stand near the stove
must warm up
stretch the bones

imagination surrounded by barbed wire

the tongue dreams:

poetry's like picking up bread crumbs
I'm Tongue, it clicked,
clapped,
& slept.

born
to laugh, a-
wakened to zombie
life (whisper, the shadow's
swallowing itself!),
surrounded by dogs
that are untrainable,
alone, trained
though untrainable
leave the classroom!
born of laughter
to a laughable
life, a life worth laughing;
something strange
rustled & buzzed, unnecessary
                    for a full breath
breath is love
breath is hard work
they lopped & chopped
                    firewood
when the state's not there
neither are you, in a state
of flux

in a place full of mice
                                    the zombie
bit his own hand
& then he felt
                    the deficits
in his dentures

2.

simple messages
it's warm
it's cold
Jura asks
if I have a tissue
then he blows a bloody snot
& goes to hock a loogie
into the stove

after cutting off
cultural heritage
because the culture creamed
.   unexcitedly
warmth
cold
without a cultural heritage
            & a birthplace
                without your own tongue
of things & causes
            I at a crossroads

because there is still
what is not I,
I is
I autonomous
without rhetoric

& then you,
as I ,
you will find
            no
            boundary

3.

    I thought
    that there were boundaries
    & I was happy

because I knew
it was just a thought:
badsector

like a sudden
whiff of shit
in the crisp
mountain
air,

soaked in the scent of centeno joven

& you get to
watch one
of the most beautiful
               historias de amor
which the cinema
          won't shoot

and Edmund & Mary Jane
          tango
          with django

aloft
in a cart
          oaked
          with aire!

APPLEMA

was pissing, with his can
to the canister, a fart
to tweak
its faint flame.
- - -
Damn it!
Heart rampage!
The sciatic nerve
like holy smoke!
A real wolf
has broken into the market!
FOR
a tausend years
we'll set up a journal
CARRÁMBA
and publish
        interviews with doggies & mousies
        en el lenguaje de perro
        y el lenguaje de ratón
        squeak squeak
        woof woof
        CARRÁMBA
        será la última palabra
        en el mundo
        muchas matas
        el lenguaje de plantas
        el lenguaje de bacterias
        BACTERIAN

the highest
state of mind
is   keine Ahnung

in the tiled stove of imagination
Professor von Absurd
burned all the libraries
crumbled the stone inscriptions
& turned the remnants into
                              a sandbox
to which he crawled
                                        babbling happily
            the clock hands twirled back time
            like a girl's hair
            & a rainbow rose from his forehead
the end of which disappeared
behind a distant planet
                        grand
                              like the sun

& he said:

since I've survived thought,
it's time to ignore civilizations

4. when we all do it together

when money & countries disappear from everyday life

trees will grow on the wrecks
of forgotten cars

the buildings will be where they are
& we

shall visit each other in our own homes
for which no one will want anything from us
we'll happily prepare warm meals

there will be love on the street

the truth will be nice

II.

A New Tristan Tzara Urgently Needed

Trash Route

—for Paweł Markowski

why aren't there
any ideas when you're on your ass why
when I sit in a chair everything dissipates
& why when I walk it's rad

a fucking bird dies!

he surfed on & off the net
let poetry be the result of a conversation
& not lonely rummaging in language
poetry erased of all its frasal funktions
poetry as mere gesture & facial expression
I envy birds

like this title, trash route
death route, death march is out
so sit tight
asswipe

just sit tight for a few ticks
I haven't jumped out the window yet
if you write, you're alive
now I'm Różewicz[13]
pushing daisies

---

[13] Tadeusz Różewicz (1921–2014), a renowned Polish poet, playwright, writer and translator who served in the Polish Home Army during World War II. His writings have been widely translated and numerous plays have been produced in New York and elsewhere.

why does this fiend[14] have so many problems
with functions & renovations
he'd better give up the past of the language
nightmarealism, you
trrr trrr tweet tweet

let's unwaste the meeting
palms, book parties
palms & psalms
the book editorial process
editing & proofreading
the processes of funding
ding fun, swing & swank
franke danke
trrr trrr tweet tweet
freak

my philosophy & logic run amok
I'm a trash man from the land o' yuck
my sour stank keeps everyone at bay
even the squatters will turn me away
I take a detour from the trash collection
my legs decide to make an objection
I, a joyful hobo, wino
pander & gander!

my laughter thru acute pain
for the government is a stain
to the government I'm a drain
a fucking bane!

---

[14] The Polish word *bies*, which is what appears in the original, is an archaic term for devil, demon or fiend. It also happens to be the surname a contemporary Polish poet, Marcin Bies, who lives in Mikołów, Upper Silesia.

(are the police calling? no one's calling . . .)

Polish tradition
& y'all traditions
come along on my mission
inside the head
of an "individual"

my head is a safe haven
for European thought
with empty strife
in life

JOIN & JOINT:

free-willer,
I'm seeking
a less capacious form

what's a poe'm
if it ain't changed its author
the miracle of self-destruktion

trapped in advertising
they want to ban the bonds
shut everything down
shut your mouth
oh, the miracle of work
in zoopolis

countrymen, you
didn't see me
put my head in the oven
to burn my hair

let others contemplate the cosmos, kick
themselves to get out of this life with dignity, because,
because I'm just getting up, stretching my arms
with a grin on my ugly mug,
undermining
here's to a good friend & a nice colleague &

I did me
a Prague-therapy, the wind whistled
thru holes in the brain, it went to get some air &
came back happier
quoth Meathead, some Lebanese blonde was there too,
a man with a glazed mind
until the tree doctors came
with transfromations

once
I discovered that I'm a crank
that I'm an ass
the darkness got frisky around the lamps
moths rose from bran & danced around the mustache
a white carriage with white horses danced with the pavement
rub your eyes

when an eyelash fell on a fly's wing
off a spider's thread tied to a finger in a tram
& hung from a wild rose's twig
in the rust of the dawn, from the morning glory, a half-
beer-later vision, oh, the homeless end of the night

on a stiff back
of the tracers of a new architecture

HELLO

my name is—
call me—of
myself a shadow,
        no stutters
smacks & claps,
when the telegraph stop
announces to the eyes
the final frame of the
message & whip logic,

when a flash of thought dilutes the
darkness & a branded bag
holds a cloth sack

TRASH ROUTE (RECYCLING)

why aren't there any
ideas when you're on your ass & when
I'm walking, a bird dies & mixes with vats
of thoughts, a rotating dustbin
like a leaky hourglass,
legs torn off lumbago
bending down is a storm
I'm a storm when
cars are cages for people
in the age of electronic conversation,
in the age of people looking away
walking away from each other more rapidly

only perhaps at a market stall
full of vegetables
a joke disinterested in intrigue

THE CENTER

is, the self
from the bottom, a polygon
of lights in a polygon
of lights, the self like
an empty glass,
setting the self in a space
that exceeds the pull
of Earth's gravity, the self
like the electronically-tuned
sound of a vibraphone bar;

how to answer a question
which is like a spring for the self, the spelunking
of the self, maybe like a rubber wall for the self, thought
like a skateboard (*oh, he fell on
his ass*)
the center's everywhere,
every particle is the center,

how to think when it's cold,
when in math
only geometry makes sense,
human geometry,

when a person's constantly
reduced to something, for
example, reduced to money,
ground zero of money, what can the marriage

of money & mercy accomplish,
what's the point of writing if it carry
a command; from which side

the guttersnipe appear more clearly
                    : where a penniless
beggar rummages in the trash, or

where non-existent millions
be funneled ruthlessly
                I dreamt
                                by
mathematics.

(a layered I?
forgiven of passion

more "unshakable" than the earth)

I beyond picture & sound

I beyond writing

I twitches

isthmus
to the unexplored

& what you've seeked,
thinkers prophets

teachers of the invisible

discover find outfigure

I unshakeable when I hurts & suffers
I unshakeable when dies

    'tis this you
    (beyond gnowing
    echoing)

PREPOEM ON GIGIPOESIE

bebe
dada
fuck the letters

dazzle my frazzle

sk(r)ew the course of association
with a different notion
distantalizing

the dance of directions
the bent axles
secant of light
the photon flare
baba
dede

letters only
encucumber
delite

CONFESSION OF A SCREWEE

to screw me like this
my own lang
& this culture
& those who speak
with this julep
& intonations
& idiolects
don't you break it

but I gots to
get away
somewheres

because instead of fountains
my thoughts be gutters

I'mma write in American

the tire tread

grind on a pebble
it's stuck in the asphalt

the hum of the tire
tunes in
the soprano aria

we sit in a room
I'm a womanizer
he's a manizer

unless it's only oceanic
rumors

he suppose to write in American
& it make me laugh
laughter that get stuck in the tongue
& grind me the oval
of my polished enamel
between the residue
of teeth

the aria thumps & thumps
soothing homeless ears

saying goodbye to youth with laughter
laughter that's better than the fist
of the American army

laughter that's better than the fist
of the Russian army

fart at the Ministry
of National Defense

now know why

it's the element that wins

Footnote to Karasek[15]

at a weedy stadium
we reminisced about a bottle

the mind encrusted in another epoch
searches for a fount in the new one

sometimes a man's so wise
that he gets tongue-tied

spirit of a time past
don't wave at me from the depths

there's no space between words
only ants marching thru the brain

look for poetry under skirts
in the bar of memory visit the basement

oh, guardian of your own ashes
cigar smoke fills the poem

the heavens aren't silent
if you have them in you

---

[15] Krzysztof Karasek (b.1937), Polish poet based in Warsaw.

illuminobjects

let every word be a revelation!
let it be beautiful like shitting under a tree,
& fucking squatting down & not
on this disgusting can. Who
will forbid me, who will tell me what to do?
My fingers smell of metal.
The smell of sweat & iron. That's
the workers' smell! The smell of electricians!
This isn't Hugo Boss! Get lost, Calvin Klein!
In *Literatura na Świecie*[16] , they think intensively about New Yorkers!
And I'm sitting who knows where! O'Hara's shmara,
shmara & samara! Kirał who? Kirał who
phthalic carbomide & chlorinated rubber?
In these circles, no one will compete with my lacerated brain,
meanwhile, I set here in the park, all a-cleans'd & the sun it's out
behind them bushes . . .

---

[16] *Literatura na Świecie* [Literature of the World] is an influential Polish literary journal that began in 1971, and which organizes each issue around a particular theme or focus. The poetry of the New York School has had a visible influence on its editors and some contributors.

Splat star

—for Marcin Ostrychacz

shoots! toot
the horn! la chispa! el poeta!
the nucleus of the self!
sound typhoon! thought tornado! if
you're me & I be you,
the impersonal me, I am is,
then your friend I aim to be,
from Spanish *desear* or
to wish.

Różewicz Akbar

beggars asking for alms
test our humanity

by saying nothing, I proclaim my existential fall
the thought of modern man must break thru the roar of information

there's something on the windowsill
that looks like mouse shit

there was no conversation that would lead somewhere
at the end of the boiled self

the age of the horse has run its course

International House of Panhandlers

where we're at
is where we've shat

our turf is marked
by where we've barfed

whatever's in the bin
we dig in

where we were born
is all shrubs & thorns

where we slept together
the city's sewage festers

we only go to those joints
where you can scam a pint

just to piss it out in the grass
a six-foot valley of ashes

am I fetching
as a man who's socially engaged?

will my attire
attract the opposite sex?

ah, like a metal shaving to a magnet,
my hand is already drawn to this trash bin

what do you want from me,
cigarette butts & scraps?

can't you see I'm socially engaged?
this fashion is such a thrill, ah

why does it hurt, auch,
if I am socially engaged?

but how can you make a quick buck on this fashion
when there's no home, where is my home?

maybe I'll end up a nationalist
it's the fashion, isn't it?

god, you've made me a Pole
& I love me some stateless anarchy

jesus socrates & buddha
also dodged social security

& traipsed where they wanted
they turned right, then turned left

& no one told them what the fuck
to do

it's cool to be socially engaged
you can sunbathe by the river

during the working hours
of the controlled majority

& think to yourself that a modern man
is held by the rein like a country horse

& there's only one command
for this horseman: giddy up!

POETRY TRAINING FILE

fingers like stalactites above the keyboard
no longer waving your hand like crocheting
your fingers running over the keyboard, the hand
like a prisoner escaping from the casemate of the self,

Baczewski's[17] pen in the moss by the canal,
no longer a thought nor a dream, hallucination, be gone,
not some thought filtered thru the community
nor the scratch of a nib in the life-death ring

only emptiness which drives the hand/s towards writing,
but why, for what, for whom, actually
it's no different than the desire to beget a child
who could be at least a little bit better

than the procreators, with this stupid hope,
that the thing which will see the light of day or night, no matter,

but that it will be more perfect than us by at least one percent:
fairer, nicer, more accurate & comforting

like the barrel of a gun pointed at the temple
(self-censorship is worse than suicide)

---

[17] Marek Krystian Emanuel Baczewski (b. 1964), a Polish poet who lives in Zawiercie.

I look at myself from a geological perspective.
Necrophiles aren't interested in the history of the species.

The Head of State with a rainbow mohawk,
latex pants & a lace Łowicz jacket,

meets with the Präsident der Stadt in Auschwitz
prison garb at the techno event in Stary Licheń.

Poles have long hanged Jaruzelski[18] & Kiszczak[19]
on the gallows in front of the Palace of Culture & Science.

Priests have given their cars away to the poorest
& started growing marijuana in the parish gardens.

Comedians with the faces of celebrities became
hermit philosophers, eating vegetables from garbage cans.

The dailies have disappeared from the windows of disheveled kiosks.
No smile will mask the high fever.

---

[18] Wojciech Jaruzelski (1923–2014), controversial former Polish president and de facto dictator during the 1980s Communist regime who instituted martial law in 1981.

[19] Czesław Kiszczak (1925–2015), powerful former interior minister in charge of the police force, the secret police and the supervision of local governments, who later became prime minister under Wojciech Jaruzelski.

LOCOMOTIVE SIRENS

look at the heart of the cathedral which is the stained-glass window
a locomotive siren floating outside the city

titmouse tit magpie blackbirds & rooks
pecking crow nuts from under the snow

like smog slog kiss-kiss side-step & jump over the track!
he missed the wall because he chickened out

the mouth's menace whistled but no wave came
the trees absorb sound concrete in a rust burrito

the liner booth barrier red lights clatter
the steady metal rhythm of the plates

POETRY LESSON
(the singing of Czech birds)

Doodly-do. Doodly-do.
Tu tu didellyllytutu.
Alloo-alloo.
K-seek.
Tu tu didelylytutu.

Jeep! Jeep! Cirvid, cirvid!
Kick, cake. Kick cake!
Tyjupilee. Tyjupilee.
Clüe clüe clüe . . .
Gü, gü, gü!

Carrie. Caric.
Tiglets, tigleet.
Pseet! Pseet!
Kakaka. Keekeekee.
Ayeeí! Crcrcr.

CrüeCrüeCrüeCrüeCrüe!
Hoo.
Juju, juju. Dieudieu. Kiev-kiev!
Hoo.
Kfueykfee-kfee-kfee!
Hoo.

III.

ROTOROBERTEIL

I WOKE UP

& felt hunger
            for new words

                                    because to jump
over snow
            from cloud to cloud is the course
of an idealized direction
                        of precipitation
on
a decrepit diamond

                                    the sky
above the dried-up dreams
of my wooden-hearted fellows

                        . . . alleviation
comes from bar bums, a festival of mustaches!! the gray beard
of a patriarch   a banjoist with
a face hewn with the wrinkles of cigarette butts
to be rolling a joint gracefully off a cliff

                                    of a pub . . .

when I'm old
I'll be a vending machine that sells cigarettes
or a one-armed bandit,   when

Mimesis knocks at the window
demanding crumbs
            for its death,

break the mirror, speak

in a snowy

whistle,

look out,
fool,

check yourself! Without a mirror
check yourself! Outside the window

your self is hanging in the air!

You're no more than dust on a stained glass!

A LUSION OF WORK
OF PERE GRINATION

A CUIRASSIER

a mermaid swam away into the depth of the sea
lay down your weapon where your eyes meet

the bell of sleep calls me from . . .
the snow-topped memory, the inhale
was thrice illegal-l-l-l,
ll,

memento mori after forty
I look at my lightly spoilt peers
how a cracked teapot can mill self-awareness;
I want to bestow (blow! blow!) awareness on porcelain!
let's play the kettle like the trumpet
let's push a whirlwind down a clarinet! yeah!

a furnished Home-Man
is walking down the street, bent over
wearing his entire closet A NEW SISYPHUS

foreskin cheese instead of feta

a space cowboy picks experiences like flowers from a meadow,
lowers his flight, smoothly floating from the ceiling to the table
his gold & turquoise collided & thru his coat-tail
merged with the spine of the universe

       … The Master of Fuck-If-I-Know
       responds to every question
       with a helpless shrug

October in Anuary

       a harmony of thoughts
       nothing but the isis sinusoids
       you went back a few
       thousand years-s

despite the sound intensifying
the mind is silent

a dinosaur in a pyramid
the roar of pyramids

the circles have wooled out . . .

       a tiny zen

               parahoney, parabrass

feints-zigzags, kung-fu & tango?!

To save an object from the trash bin.
To train the brain with a word.

Please revise your remark:

the self is puking

everything inside me is puking

the logo   with   the letter   f   logo logo

The word is puking

puking at human thought

at the thinking practice
a puke for the cause
a puke for the result

puke like frost flowers on a windowpane

The word pukes with the fractal loco loco

the dead are over

the barf & hiccups

1.
at the edge of a stall   .   a dirty smile
                                                  dirty & in twilight

an instant soup of words

and:

I call words with my thought
like sacks in an aerodynamic tunnel
doesn't matter
it's the world's prison yard
tenderly embraced with an abstract consciousness
& a pure laugh without lungs or mouth

so many books about humanity
works about the human plight
& there are eyes that look at our species
the way we look at ants

a pile of mulch
a population not worth a damn

I call words with my thought
a pure abstraction
I imagine it
as a plastic aperture on the cosmos
no movement

as if I were looking at the cosmos
from outside the cosmos
as if it were a dust bunny
from an unimaginable distance
tho everything's down
to a contour

why should I speak & write
if I'm calling words
I'm calling wordlessly
only by paying attention
to the unknown
& that's enough for me
because it exists

there, even the static of thoughts
is disruptive

1. Knowledge

everything has its axis
its circle & is individual

some rules for existence
in any form

        have their axis their circle
        & are individual, tho

        nameless & boundless
        what speaks to us, humans

        to our interior, which
        has its axis its circle

        & is individual & is
        the greatest mystery

        what's hiding behind
        the interior, a trapdoor to

        another world, where
        even the greatest doubt

        is an unnecessary activity
        because we don't need it, the way

        we don't need all that
        knowledge, which we snort in

        or they pump in us by force,
        throwing it down the expanse of the self,

which is our consciousness
set aglow by imagination

Acknowledgements

The author would like to thank everyone who helped him during the difficult five years in which he was homeless and working on *The Squatters' Gift*; he dedicates this collection to you:

Konrad Góra, Marta Podgórnik, Rafał Muszer, Adam Sojka, Barbara Rybicka, Petr Motýl, Ivana Motýlová, Adam Stiller, Marcin Ostrychacz, Łukasz Jaśkiewicz, Adam Sierpowski, Ivana Machová, Adam Grzelec, Robert "Robercik" Bornikowski, Łukasz Żyła, Beata Matuszek, "Marky," Stanisław Bukowiecki, Adam Przybyła, Jacek Inglot, Jan Rossa, Didi Akao Omodi, Ewa Sonnenberg, Karol Pęcherz, Grzegorz Czekański, Łukasz Plata, Andrzej Wiśnik, Ilona Król, Basník Ticho, Anatolia "Tosia" Wiśniewska, Jiři Machaček, Josef Straka, Katarzyna Mielcarek, Adam Wiedemann, Michał Perła, Miłosz Biedrzycki, Zbigniew Libera, Mariola Przyjemska, Adrian Mrowicki, Maciej Melecki, Dawid Mateusz, Radosław Gacka, Peter Biskup, Małgorzata Oczak, Olga Geppert, Iga Michalska, Michał Strycharczyk, Andrzej Trybulski, Ivan Motýl, Mariusz Grzebalski, Marek Wdowicz, Ondra Volk, Ida Bubnel, Wojciech Bonowicz, "Tommy," Maria Magdalena Beszterda, Ewa Wachowiak, Janoš Jesensky, Agata Patralska-Obarewicz, Ivo Slavik, Tomasz "Świstak" Rogalski, Andrzej Kamiński, Łukasz Gamrot, Dawid Koteja, Beata Gula, Vit Kremlička, Marcin Czerwiński, Adam Krotofil, Marta Rogalska, "Edmund", Dariusz Kołodziej, Monika Glosowitz, Filip Surowiak, Wiktor Wiktorski, Michał Kasprzak, Tomasz Świtalski,

Ewa Poniżnik, Jagoda Wlaźnik, Justyna Radczyńska, Petr Řehak, Jakub Řehak, Maja Staśko, Andrzej Sosnowski, "Pumba", Kamil Brewiński, Sylwia Dwornicka, Piotr Sommer, Bogumił Rybicki, Silvia Ruppeldtová, Renata Fedaková, Ivan Motýl, "Ziemniak", Grażyna Zarzecka-Czech, Adam "Beret" Mańczuk, Maria Bitka, Jacek Gutorow, Olga Tokarczuk, Sylwia Kolar, Patrycja Kopacka, Paweł Markowski, Beata Bols, Tomasz "Rogo" Rogovski, Darek Foks, Mateusz Dworek, Adam Idach, "Leo", Szymon Szwarc, Zuzanna Ogorzewska, Jerzy "Kali" Wenglarzy, Krzysztof Śliwka, Grzegorz Lerka, Grzegorz Wróblewski, Zbigniew Machej, Tomasz Żarnecki, "Czacha", Andrij Bondar, Anna Targiel, Maciej Krynicki, Marie Čmělikóva, Marian Bednarek, Grzegorz Walczak, Seweryn Górczak, Monika Błaszczak, Halina Smyczek, Sławomir "Baron" Stężały, Bohdan Zadura, Gabriela Pienias, Marcin Bies, Ryszard Szczepanek, "Bakcyl", Przemysław Suchanecki, Szczepan Kopyt, Aleksander Larysz, Adam Borowski, Mirosław Ropiak, Vasiliy Ivanov, Jörg Piringer, Przemysław Witkowski, Leszek Onak, Piotr Żyła, Jacek Żebrowski, Piotr Sojka.

And:

the Prague collective "Cibulka", the Vienna collective "Pizzeria Anarchia," the Wroclaw Wagenburg, the Wroclaw CRK, the Poznań collective "Rozbrat," the Poznań collective "Od:Zysk," the Prague collective "Klinika," the Krakow collective "Reaktor,," the Vienna EKH, the Warsaw collective "Syrena," the Warsaw collective "Przychodnia" and Lesosquat.

And:

Staromiejski Dom Kultury, "Literatura na Świecie", Tajne Komplety, Biuro Literackie, Stowarzyszenie Pisarzy Polskich Wrocław, Kalambur, Stowarzyszenie Pisarzy Polskich Kraków, Lokator, Instytut Mikołowski, Wielkopolska Biblioteka Publiczna i Centrum Animacji Kultury, CK Zamek, Dragon, (były) GuGalander, Ars Cameralis, Fińska, Ogniwo, Dom Kultury Chwałowice, Natalia/Turbina, (A)

VOID, Paliárka, literární obtýdeník "Tvar", revue "Protimluv," kavárna Fra, Hany Bany, SALE, Café V Lese (Ostrava a Praha), Księgarnia Hiszpańska.

And:
—all the drivers who gave me a lift,
—the dogs and cats (Baretta, Ares, Benek, Nitka, Kamoro, Eliašek, Kosmos, etc.) and the piggy Grażynka.

Thank you again.

The author and translator wish to thank John O'Brien at Dalkey Archive Press for his support, trust, and gumption to take on this project. Special thanks for Will Evans and Chad Post for seeing the project through. We would also like to thank the editors of *Anomaly*, *Asymptote*, and *Periodicities*, where significant excerpts from this book first appeared (sometimes in earlier versions). Particular thanks to Anna Rosenwong, rob mclennan, and Garrett Phelps for their early and enthusiastic support of this work.

The translator would like to express his gratitude to the people who helped push him towards the finish line in various ways during the many days and months that a comma or collocation kept him awake: Ray Bianchi, Patt & Walter Grey, Jarek Hetman, Ela Kotkowska, Sarah Mangold, Dominick Mastrangelo, Bronka Nowicka, and Laura Wetherington—thank you for your friendship, time and effort, and words of encouragement. A special thanks to Paulina Ambroży and Krzysztof Majer for their meticulous reading of and helpful comments on a draft of the manuscript, and to Anastasia Nikolis for her astute copy edits.

Finally, the translator would like to extend his deepest gratitude to his wife, Katarzyna Szuster-Tardi, for her invaluable input, generosity, humor, patience, creativity, and example. She valiantly saved more than a few eagles from being slaughtered on a balloon.

ROBERT 'RYBA' RYBICKI was born in Rybnik in 1976. A poet, translator, squatter (at times), and self-described 'happener,' Rybicki is the author of nine books of poetry, including *Epifanie i katatonie* [Epiphanies & Catatonics], *Masakra kalaczakra* [Kalachakra massacre], and a collected volume, *Podręcznik naukowy dla onironautów* [A Scientific Handbook for Oneironauts]. He served as the former editor of the artistic magazine Plama in Rybnik as well as the Polish weekly Nowy Czas [New Time] in London. His collection *Dar Meneli* [The Squatters' Gift] was the winner of the Juliusz Upper Silesian Literary Award in 2018. He currently lives in Kraków and organizes literary events there.

MARK TARDI is the author of *The Circus of Trust* (Dalkey Archive Press, 2017), *Airport music*, and *Euclid Shudders*. *Prologue*, an award-winning cinepoem collaboration with Polish multimedia artist Adam Mańkowski, has been screened at film festivals throughout Europe and the United States. Recent work and translations have appeared or are forthcoming in *Circumference*, *Denver Quarterly*, *Berlin Quarterly*, *Paraphrasis*, *Notre Dame Review*, *Asymptote*, *Anomaly*, and *Periodicities*. He was a writer-in-residence at MASS MoCA in January 2020 and will be a research fellow at the Harry Ransom Center in 2021. A former Fulbright scholar, he is on faculty at the University of Łódź.

MICHAL AJVAZ, *The Golden Age.*
The Other City.
PIERRE ALBERT-BIROT, *Grabinoulor.*
YUZ ALESHKOVSKY, *Kangaroo.*
FELIPE ALFAU, *Chromos.*
Locos.
JOE AMATO, *Samuel Taylor's Last Night.*
IVAN ÂNGELO, *The Celebration.*
The Tower of Glass.
ANTÓNIO LOBO ANTUNES, *Knowledge of Hell.*
The Splendor of Portugal.
ALAIN ARIAS-MISSON, *Theatre of Incest.*
JOHN ASHBERY & JAMES SCHUYLER, *A Nest of Ninnies.*
ROBERT ASHLEY, *Perfect Lives.*
GABRIELA AVIGUR-ROTEM, *Heatwave and Crazy Birds.*
DJUNA BARNES, *Ladies Almanack.*
Ryder.
JOHN BARTH, *Letters.*
Sabbatical.
DONALD BARTHELME, *The King.*
Paradise.
SVETISLAV BASARA, *Chinese Letter.*
MIQUEL BAUÇÀ, *The Siege in the Room.*
RENÉ BELLETTO, *Dying.*
MAREK BIENCZYK, *Transparency.*
ANDREI BITOV, *Pushkin House.*
ANDREJ BLATNIK, *You Do Understand.*
Law of Desire.
LOUIS PAUL BOON, *Chapel Road.*
My Little War.
Summer in Termuren.
ROGER BOYLAN, *Killoyle.*
IGNÁCIO DE LOYOLA BRANDÃO, *Anonymous Celebrity.*
Zero.
BONNIE BREMSER, *Troia: Mexican Memoirs.*
CHRISTINE BROOKE-ROSE, *Amalgamemnon.*
BRIGID BROPHY, *In Transit.*
The Prancing Novelist.

GERALD L. BRUNS, *Modern Poetry and the Idea of Language.*
GABRIELLE BURTON, *Heartbreak Hotel.*
MICHEL BUTOR, *Degrees.*
Mobile.
G. CABRERA INFANTE, *Infante's Inferno.*
Three Trapped Tigers.
JULIETA CAMPOS, *The Fear of Losing Eurydice.*
ANNE CARSON, *Eros the Bittersweet.*
ORLY CASTEL-BLOOM, *Dolly City.*
LOUIS-FERDINAND CÉLINE, *North.*
Conversations with Professor Y.
London Bridge.
MARIE CHAIX, *The Laurels of Lake Constance.*
HUGO CHARTERIS, *The Tide Is Right.*
ERIC CHEVILLARD, *Demolishing Nisard.*
The Author and Me.
MARC CHOLODENKO, *Mordechai Schamz.*
JOSHUA COHEN, *Witz.*
EMILY HOLMES COLEMAN, *The Shutter of Snow.*
ERIC CHEVILLARD, *The Author and Me.*
ROBERT COOVER, *A Night at the Movies.*
STANLEY CRAWFORD, *Log of the S.S.*
The Mrs Unguentine.
Some Instructions to My Wife.
RENÉ CREVEL, *Putting My Foot in It.*
RALPH CUSACK, *Cadenza.*
NICHOLAS DELBANCO, *Sherbrookes.*
The Count of Concord.
NIGEL DENNIS, *Cards of Identity.*
PETER DIMOCK, *A Short Rhetoric for Leaving the Family.*
ARIEL DORFMAN, *Konfidenz.*
COLEMAN DOWELL, *Island People.*
Too Much Flesh and Jabez.
ARKADII DRAGOMOSHCHENKO, *Dust.*
RIKKI DUCORNET, *Phosphor in Dreamland.*
The Complete Butcher's Tales.

RIKKI DUCORNET (cont.), *The Jade Cabinet.*
The Fountains of Neptune.

WILLIAM EASTLAKE, *The Bamboo Bed.*
Castle Keep.
Lyric of the Circle Heart.

JEAN ECHENOZ, *Chopin's Move.*

STANLEY ELKIN, *A Bad Man.*
Criers and Kibitzers, Kibitzers and Criers.
The Dick Gibson Show.
The Franchiser.
The Living End.
Mrs. Ted Bliss.

FRANÇOIS EMMANUEL, *Invitation to a Voyage.*

PAUL EMOND, *The Dance of a Sham.*

SALVADOR ESPRIU, *Ariadne in the Grotesque Labyrinth.*

LESLIE A. FIEDLER, *Love and Death in the American Novel.*

JUAN FILLOY, *Op Oloop.*

ANDY FITCH, *Pop Poetics.*

GUSTAVE FLAUBERT, *Bouvard and Pécuchet.*

KASS FLEISHER, *Talking out of School.*

JON FOSSE, *Aliss at the Fire.*
Melancholy.

FORD MADOX FORD, *The March of Literature.*

MAX FRISCH, *I'm Not Stiller.*
Man in the Holocene.

CARLOS FUENTES, *Christopher Unborn.*
Distant Relations.
Terra Nostra.
Where the Air Is Clear.

TAKEHIKO FUKUNAGA, *Flowers of Grass.*

WILLIAM GADDIS, JR., *The Recognitions.*

JANICE GALLOWAY, *Foreign Parts.*
The Trick Is to Keep Breathing.

WILLIAM H. GASS, *Life Sentences.*
The Tunnel.
The World Within the Word.
Willie Masters' Lonesome Wife.

GÉRARD GAVARRY, *Hoppla! 1 2 3.*

ETIENNE GILSON, *The Arts of the Beautiful.*
Forms and Substances in the Arts.

C. S. GISCOMBE, *Giscome Road.*
Here.

DOUGLAS GLOVER, *Bad News of the Heart.*

WITOLD GOMBROWICZ, *A Kind of Testament.*

PAULO EMÍLIO SALES GOMES, *P's Three Women.*

GEORGI GOSPODINOV, *Natural Novel.*

JUAN GOYTISOLO, *Count Julian.*
Juan the Landless.
Makbara.
Marks of Identity.

HENRY GREEN, *Blindness.*
Concluding.
Doting.
Nothing.

JACK GREEN, *Fire the Bastards!*

JIŘÍ GRUŠA, *The Questionnaire.*

MELA HARTWIG, *Am I a Redundant Human Being?*

JOHN HAWKES, *The Passion Artist.*
Whistlejacket.

ELIZABETH HEIGHWAY, ED., *Contemporary Georgian Fiction.*

AIDAN HIGGINS, *Balcony of Europe.*
Blind Man's Bluff.
Bornholm Night-Ferry.
Langrishe, Go Down.
Scenes from a Receding Past.

KEIZO HINO, *Isle of Dreams.*

KAZUSHI HOSAKA, *Plainsong.*

ALDOUS HUXLEY, *Antic Hay.*
Point Counter Point.
Those Barren Leaves.
Time Must Have a Stop.

NAOYUKI II, *The Shadow of a Blue Cat.*

DRAGO JANČAR, *The Tree with No Name.*

MIKHEIL JAVAKHISHVILI, *Kvachi.*

GERT JONKE, *The Distant Sound.*
Homage to Czerny.
The System of Vienna.

FOR A FULL LIST OF PUBLICATIONS, VISIT: www.dalkeyarchive.com

JACQUES JOUET, *Mountain R.*
Savage.
Upstaged.
MIEKO KANAI, *The Word Book.*
YORAM KANIUK, *Life on Sandpaper.*
ZURAB KARUMIDZE, *Dagny.*
JOHN KELLY, *From Out of the City.*
HUGH KENNER, *Flaubert, Joyce and Beckett: The Stoic Comedians.*
Joyce's Voices.
DANILO KIŠ, *The Attic.*
The Lute and the Scars.
Psalm 44.
A Tomb for Boris Davidovich.
ANITA KONKKA, *A Fool's Paradise.*
GEORGE KONRÁD, *The City Builder.*
TADEUSZ KONWICKI, *A Minor Apocalypse.*
The Polish Complex.
ANNA KORDZAIA-SAMADASHVILI, *Me, Margarita.*
MENIS KOUMANDAREAS, *Koula.*
ELAINE KRAF, *The Princess of 72nd Street.*
JIM KRUSOE, *Iceland.*
AYSE KULIN, *Farewell: A Mansion in Occupied Istanbul.*
EMILIO LASCANO TEGUI, *On Elegance While Sleeping.*
ERIC LAURRENT, *Do Not Touch.*
VIOLETTE LEDUC, *La Bâtarde.*
EDOUARD LEVÉ, *Autoportrait.*
Newspaper.
Suicide.
Works.
MARIO LEVI, *Istanbul Was a Fairy Tale.*
DEBORAH LEVY, *Billy and Girl.*
JOSÉ LEZAMA LIMA, *Paradiso.*
ROSA LIKSOM, *Dark Paradise.*
OSMAN LINS, *Avalovara.*
The Queen of the Prisons of Greece.
FLORIAN LIPUŠ, *The Errors of Young Tjaž.*
GORDON LISH, *Peru.*
ALF MACLOCHLAINN, *Out of Focus.*
Past Habitual.

The Corpus in the Library.
RON LOEWINSOHN, *Magnetic Field(s).*
YURI LOTMAN, *Non-Memoirs.*
D. KEITH MANO, *Take Five.*
MINA LOY, *Stories and Essays of Mina Loy.*
MICHELINE AHARONIAN MARCOM, *A Brief History of Yes.*
The Mirror in the Well.
BEN MARCUS, *The Age of Wire and String.*
WALLACE MARKFIELD, *Teitlebaum's Window.*
DAVID MARKSON, *Reader's Block.*
Wittgenstein's Mistress.
CAROLE MASO, *AVA.*
HISAKI MATSUURA, *Triangle.*
LADISLAV MATEJKA & KRYSTYNA POMORSKA, EDS., *Readings in Russian Poetics: Formalist & Structuralist Views.*
HARRY MATHEWS, *Cigarettes.*
The Conversions.
The Human Country.
The Journalist.
My Life in CIA.
Singular Pleasures.
The Sinking of the Odradek.
Stadium.
Tlooth.
HISAKI MATSUURA, *Triangle.*
DONAL MCLAUGHLIN, *beheading the virgin mary, and other stories.*
JOSEPH MCELROY, *Night Soul and Other Stories.*
ABDELWAHAB MEDDEB, *Talismano.*
GERHARD MEIER, *Isle of the Dead.*
HERMAN MELVILLE, *The Confidence-Man.*
AMANDA MICHALOPOULOU, *I'd Like.*
STEVEN MILLHAUSER, *The Barnum Museum.*
In the Penny Arcade.
RALPH J. MILLS, JR., *Essays on Poetry.*
MOMUS, *The Book of Jokes.*
CHRISTINE MONTALBETTI, *The Origin of Man.*
Western.

NICHOLAS MOSLEY, *Accident.*
Assassins.
Catastrophe Practice.
A Garden of Trees.
Hopeful Monsters.
Imago Bird.
Inventing God.
Look at the Dark.
Metamorphosis.
Natalie Natalia.
Serpent.

WARREN MOTTE, *Fables of the Novel:*
French Fiction since 1990.
Fiction Now: The French Novel in the
21st Century.
Mirror Gazing.
Oulipo: A Primer of Potential Literature.

GERALD MURNANE, *Barley Patch.*
Inland.

YVES NAVARRE, *Our Share of Time.*
Sweet Tooth.

DOROTHY NELSON, *In Night's City.*
Tar and Feathers.

ESHKOL NEVO, *Homesick.*

WILFRIDO D. NOLLEDO, *But for*
the Lovers.

BORIS A. NOVAK, *The Master of*
Insomnia.

FLANN O'BRIEN, *At Swim-Two-Birds.*
The Best of Myles.
The Dalkey Archive.
The Hard Life.
The Poor Mouth.
The Third Policeman.

CLAUDE OLLIER, *The Mise-en-Scène.*
Wert and the Life Without End.

PATRIK OUŘEDNÍK, *Europeana.*
The Opportune Moment, 1855.

BORIS PAHOR, *Necropolis.*

FERNANDO DEL PASO, *News from*
the Empire.
Palinuro of Mexico.

ROBERT PINGET, *The Inquisitory.*
Mahu or The Material.
Trio.

MANUEL PUIG, *Betrayed by Rita*
Hayworth.

The Buenos Aires Affair.
Heartbreak Tango.

RAYMOND QUENEAU, *The Last Days.*
Odile.
Pierrot Mon Ami.
Saint Glinglin.

ANN QUIN, *Berg.*
Passages.
Three.
Tripticks.

ISHMAEL REED, *The Free-Lance*
Pallbearers.
The Last Days of Louisiana Red.
Ishmael Reed: The Plays.
Juice!
The Terrible Threes.
The Terrible Twos.
Yellow Back Radio Broke-Down.

JASIA REICHARDT, *15 Journeys Warsaw*
to London.

JOÃO UBALDO RIBEIRO, *House of the*
Fortunate Buddhas.

JEAN RICARDOU, *Place Names.*

RAINER MARIA RILKE,
The Notebooks of Malte Laurids Brigge.

JULIÁN RÍOS, *The House of Ulysses.*
Larva: A Midsummer Night's Babel.
Poundemonium.

ALAIN ROBBE-GRILLET, *Project for a*
Revolution in New York.
A Sentimental Novel.

AUGUSTO ROA BASTOS, *I the Supreme.*

DANIËL ROBBERECHTS, *Arriving in*
Avignon.

JEAN ROLIN, *The Explosion of the*
Radiator Hose.

OLIVIER ROLIN, *Hotel Crystal.*

ALIX CLEO ROUBAUD, *Alix's Journal.*

JACQUES ROUBAUD, *The Form of*
a City Changes Faster, Alas, Than the
Human Heart.
The Great Fire of London.
Hortense in Exile.
Hortense Is Abducted.
Mathematics: The Plurality of Worlds of
Lewis.
Some Thing Black.

FOR A FULL LIST OF PUBLICATIONS, VISIT: www.dalkeyarchive.com

RAYMOND ROUSSEL, *Impressions of Africa.*

VEDRANA RUDAN, *Night.*

PABLO M. RUIZ, *Four Cold Chapters on the Possibility of Literature.*

GERMAN SADULAEV, *The Maya Pill.*

TOMAŽ ŠALAMUN, *Soy Realidad.*

LYDIE SALVAYRE, *The Company of Ghosts.*
The Lecture.
The Power of Flies.

LUIS RAFAEL SÁNCHEZ, *Macho Camacho's Beat.*

SEVERO SARDUY, *Cobra & Maitreya.*

NATHALIE SARRAUTE, *Do You Hear Them?*
Martereau.
The Planetarium.

STIG SÆTERBAKKEN, *Siamese.*
Self-Control.
Through the Night.

ARNO SCHMIDT, *Collected Novellas.*
Collected Stories.
Nobodaddy's Children.
Two Novels.

ASAF SCHURR, *Motti.*

GAIL SCOTT, *My Paris.*

DAMION SEARLS, *What We Were Doing and Where We Were Going.*

JUNE AKERS SEESE, *Is This What Other Women Feel Too?*

BERNARD SHARE, *Inish.*
Transit.

VIKTOR SHKLOVSKY, *Bowstring.*
Literature and Cinematography.
Theory of Prose.
Third Factory.
Zoo, or Letters Not about Love.

PIERRE SINIAC, *The Collaborators.*

KJERSTI A. SKOMSVOLD, *The Faster I Walk, the Smaller I Am.*

JOSEF ŠKVORECKÝ, *The Engineer of Human Souls.*

GILBERT SORRENTINO, *Aberration of Starlight.*
Blue Pastoral.
Crystal Vision.

Imaginative Qualities of Actual Things.
Mulligan Stew. Red the Fiend.
Steelwork.
Under the Shadow.

MARKO SOSIČ, *Ballerina, Ballerina.*

ANDRZEJ STASIUK, *Dukla.*
Fado.

GERTRUDE STEIN, *The Making of Americans.*
A Novel of Thank You.

LARS SVENDSEN, *A Philosophy of Evil.*

PIOTR SZEWC, *Annihilation.*

GONÇALO M. TAVARES, *A Man: Klaus Klump.*
Jerusalem.
Learning to Pray in the Age of Technique.

LUCIAN DAN TEODOROVICI, *Our Circus Presents...*

NIKANOR TERATOLOGEN, *Assisted Living.*

STEFAN THEMERSON, *Hobson's Island.*
The Mystery of the Sardine.
Tom Harris.

TAEKO TOMIOKA, *Building Waves.*

JOHN TOOMEY, *Sleepwalker.*

DUMITRU TSEPENEAG, *Hotel Europa.*
The Necessary Marriage.
Pigeon Post.
Vain Art of the Fugue.

ESTHER TUSQUETS, *Stranded.*

DUBRAVKA UGRESIC, *Lend Me Your Character.*
Thank You for Not Reading.

TOR ULVEN, *Replacement.*

MATI UNT, *Brecht at Night.*
Diary of a Blood Donor.
Things in the Night.

ÁLVARO URIBE & OLIVIA SEARS, EDS., *Best of Contemporary Mexican Fiction.*

ELOY URROZ, *Friction.*
The Obstacles.

LUISA VALENZUELA, *Dark Desires and the Others.*
He Who Searches.

PAUL VERHAEGHEN, *Omega Minor.*

BORIS VIAN, *Heartsnatcher.*

LLORENÇ VILLALONGA, *The Dolls' Room.*

TOOMAS VINT, *An Unending Landscape.*

ORNELA VORPSI, *The Country Where No One Ever Dies.*

AUSTRYN WAINHOUSE, *Hedyphagetica.*

CURTIS WHITE, *America's Magic Mountain.*
The Idea of Home.
Memories of My Father Watching TV.
Requiem.

DIANE WILLIAMS,
Excitability: Selected Stories.
Romancer Erector.

DOUGLAS WOOLF, *Wall to Wall.*
Ya! & John-Juan.

JAY WRIGHT, *Polynomials and Pollen.*
The Presentable Art of Reading Absence.

PHILIP WYLIE, *Generation of Vipers.*

MARGUERITE YOUNG, *Angel in the Forest.*
Miss MacIntosh, My Darling.

REYOUNG, *Unbabbling.*

VLADO ŽABOT, *The Succubus.*

ZORAN ŽIVKOVIĆ , *Hidden Camera.*

LOUIS ZUKOFSKY, *Collected Fiction.*

VITOMIL ZUPAN, *Minuet for Guitar.*

SCOTT ZWIREN, *God Head.*

AND MORE . . .